Strange Fruit

BILLIE HOLIDAY AND THE POWER OF A PROTEST SONG

GARY GOLIO

illustrated by
CHARLOTTE RILEY-WEBB

MILLBROOK PRESS
Minneapolis

TO ABEL, BILLIE, BARNEY, AND THEIR
VISION OF A BETTER WORLD
—G.G.

TO MY 104-YEAR-OLD GODMOTHER,
LELIA WILLIAMS, WHO HAS
SURVIVED HER OWN "STRANGE
FRUIT" ERA AND EMERGED
VICTORIOUS!
—C.R.W.

Author's Acknowledgments

Personal thanks to Robert Meeropol, for speaking to me about his father, Abel Meeropol, and for providing insights into the writing of "Strange Fruit." Additional thanks to Dr. Rosita M. Sands, Professor of Music, Columbia College Chicago, for offering invaluable feedback on the text.

Millbrook Press
A division of Lerner Publishing Group, Inc.
241 First Avenue North
Minneapolis, MN 55401 USA

For reading levels and more information, look up this title at www.lernerbooks.com.

The photo of Billie Holiday is used with the permission of the Library of Congress.

Designed by Danielle Carnito.
Main body text set in Palatino Sans LT Pro Regular 14/18. Typeface provided by Linotype AG.
The illustrations in this book were created with acrylic paint and tissue collage on canvas paper.

Library of Congress Cataloging-in-Publication Data

Names: Golio, Gary author. | Riley-Webb, Charlotte illustrator.
Title: Strange fruit : Billie Holiday and the power of a protest song / Gary Golio ; illustrated by Charlotte Riley-Webb.
Description: Minneapolis : Millbrook Press, [2017] | Includes bibliographical references. | Description based on print version record and CIP data provided by publisher; resource not viewed.
Identifiers: LCCN 2016020046 (print) | LCCN 2016019763 (ebook) | ISBN 9781512428377 (eb pdf) | ISBN 9781467751230 (lb : alk. paper)
Subjects: LCSH: Holiday, Billie, 1915–1959—Juvenile literature. | Allan, Lewis, 1903–1986. Strange fruit—Juvenile literature. | Lynching—United States—History—Juvenile literature.
Classification: LCC ML3930.H64 (print) | LCC ML3930.H64 G65 2017 (ebook) | DDC 782.42165—dc23

LC record available at https://lccn.loc.gov/2016020046

Manufactured in the United States of America
1-36611-17193-6/27/2016

Somebody once said
we never know what is enough
until we know what's
more than enough.
BILLIE HOLIDAY

This time, Billie'd had enough.

Sure, she was grateful. Grateful for her incredible singing voice. Grateful, at 23, to have worked with some of the finest jazz musicians in the country. Grateful for a few hit records that made her more well known and able to get better jobs.

And grateful to Artie Shaw, for hiring her as one of the first black singers to work in an all-white band.

But then everything changed.

Billie was singing in New York City's
famous Blue Room, at the Hotel Lincoln.

First, the staff told her not to talk with the
customers. Then they said she couldn't walk around by herself,
because someone might think that black people were staying at the hotel.
She even had to use the service elevator so guests wouldn't see her, and walk
through the kitchen to get to the stage. Worst of all was being kept upstairs in a
small room before showtime so she wouldn't cause any trouble.

Why? Because Billie was furious. And she blamed Artie for not taking her side.

Enough had finally become *too much.*

So she quit.

Billie had already seen more than her share of hard times.

As a baby, she'd been left with an older half sister by her mother, who was gone for years.

At 10, she ended up in a reform school for colored girls, all because of a terrible thing done to *her*.

And when she finally moved to New York City to be with her mother, they were both arrested, and Billie sent to jail. She was only 14.

Those early years were rough, but what kept her going was music and especially a love of *jazz*.

All she wanted to do was sing.

Billie wasn't going to scrub floors like her mother. She had a plan to *be* somebody.

Jobs in small cafes led to work in nightclubs around New York City. In one place, the audience loved Billie's voice so much they threw money right onto the floor.

It was a bright beginning.

At just 15, Billie was hired at a popular Harlem music club. Moving from table to table, she began singing each song differently every time. Listening to the trumpet and saxophone, she started *improvising*—using her voice to play with the melody and lyrics. She was going beyond words and, like the other musicians, her singing had more to say than just notes on the page.

This was the
heart of jazz.

Now those who heard her said she sounded like nobody else.

But being in the spotlight wasn't easy.

Light-skinned Billie once had to put on dark makeup because she looked too *white* for an all-black band. Another time, white bandmates painted a red dot on her forehead—to make her look like a woman from India—just so she could stay at the same hotel with them instead of sleeping on the tour bus.

Laws separating whites and blacks made things tough for Billie wherever she went. In some places, she might have been killed for even standing next to a white person, onstage or off.

She dreamed of having a place to work where she could perform with anyone she wanted and everyone could listen to her sing.

Two months after leaving Artie's band, Billie got her wish.

In December of 1938, an unusual new club was set to open in New York City. It was the creation of Barney Josephson, a one-time shoe salesman from New Jersey.

Barney had visited Harlem's famous Cotton Club, where the greatest black entertainers in the country performed. He loved the noise and excitement as much as the music. What he *didn't* love was that black people weren't allowed to sit at the tables or to be customers at all. Here in the middle of a black neighborhood was a club meant only for white people. This didn't seem right to Barney, and he decided to do something about it.

So on the night before New Year's Eve, Barney opened his own club in Greenwich Village, called Cafe Society. And not only was it open to black customers, but it gave them the best seats in the house.

Now black people could see white *and* black performers from the front of the club, closest to the stage. There was nothing like it—not in New York City and maybe not in the whole country.

Early on, Barney had asked Billie to sing at Cafe Society and hired top-notch musicians to back her up. She and the club became an immediate success.

Then Barney got a visit from Abel Meeropol, a high school teacher and songwriter. The son of Jewish immigrants, Abel was outraged by the ongoing racism and violence against American Negroes. Haunted for days by a photo he'd seen, he took up his pen and wrote something called "Strange Fruit."

It was a song about lynching.

When Billie first heard Abel sing "Strange Fruit" for her, she was unimpressed. The song wasn't jazz and it wasn't really blues, and what did the word *pastoral* mean, anyway?

But Barney thought the song was important, and Billie believed in what Cafe Society stood for. She agreed to try out the song— if only as a favor to Barney.

Studying the words, Billie thought about her father, a jazz musician who died after being turned away from a whites-only hospital. But what would *other* people make of the song?

At a party in Harlem, Billie sang "Strange Fruit." Her voice, with Abel's words.

Everyone in the apartment became quiet, and the smiles left their faces.

Billie had her answer.

At the club, Barney told Billie that "Strange Fruit" would be the last song in her set, with no encores to follow. When it was over, she'd quietly leave the stage.

That night, waiters froze in place. People stopped talking, and the room was dimmed to near darkness.

Southern trees bear a strange fruit, blood on the leaves and blood at the root

Some people in the audience looked uncomfortable or just confused.

Why was there blood on the leaves of a tree?

What exactly was this song about?

A few people nearly got up from their seats and left.

As Billie continued singing, her face became more expressive. At times, she looked tortured, angry, or sad. Her voice pierced the air. The last few words—about a strange and bitter crop—sounded more like a cry of pain

Then the spotlight went out,

and Billie was gone.

For a few moments,

there was nothing

but silence.

Finally, one person slowly began clapping, followed by another, until the entire room exploded in applause as the audience rose to its feet.

Backstage, Billie took a long, deep breath.

From that day on, "Strange Fruit" would scorch the minds and hearts of those who heard it. Billie would be cursed, threatened, and assaulted for singing "that song" in clubs and concert halls throughout the country. She'd tell her worried mother that performing "Strange Fruit" *might make things better,* even though she knew that black people had been killed for less.

"But you'll be dead," her mother said. To which Billie replied, **"Yeah, but I'll feel it. I'll know it in my grave."**

Southern trees bear a strange fruit,

Blood on the leaves and blood at the root,

Black body swinging in the Southern breeze,

Strange fruit hanging from the poplar trees.

Pastoral scene of the gallant South,

The bulging eyes and the twisted mouth,

Scent of magnolia, sweet and fresh,

And the sudden smell of burning flesh!

Here is a fruit for the crows to pluck,

For the rain to gather, for the wind to suck,

For the sun to rot, for a tree to drop,

Here is a strange and bitter crop.

WHAT HAPPENED NEXT . . .

News traveled fast after Billie debuted "Strange Fruit" in early 1939. Even before an article in *Time* magazine hit the stands, crowds filled the tables at Cafe Society to hear her sing *that song*. The publicity made Billie a star and gave her the confidence to go one step further. When her producer and record company refused to record "Strange Fruit," she turned to an independent jazz label. Released as a single (with another song on the flip side), "Strange Fruit" eventually sold one million copies. It became Billie's best-selling record as well as her signature song, even as most radio stations in America refused to play it.

From then on, Billie was often verbally or physically harassed for singing "Strange Fruit." She nevertheless insisted that it be written into her contract when performing at clubs and concert halls throughout the United States. Billie referred to "Strange Fruit" as her personal protest, and sang it as a gift to her people to voice their suffering. Close friends said that singing the song made her both sick and upset, after all she'd seen and experienced as a black woman.

Lynching is the execution—most often by hanging but also by burning or shooting—of a man, woman, or teen, by a lawless crowd or mob, without due process. *Lynching*, as a term, has uncertain origins, but is usually attributed to Charles Lynch (1736–1796), a Virginia planter and justice of the peace who held informal trials of British loyalists during the American Revolutionary War.

Between 1882 and 1939, there were nearly five thousand lynchings in the United States, with almost 75 percent of these involving black Americans. By the time Abel Meeropol wrote "Strange Fruit" and Billie sang it, the numbers had dropped considerably, though racism and oppression—both legal and social—remained widespread. Attempts to pass a federal antilynching bill in Congress would not succeed until 2005.

"Strange Fruit" brought attention to the deep-rooted problem of racism and spoke to millions of black *and* white Americans yearning for a more just and civil society. It proved to be a powerful example of protest art and galvanized what would become the civil rights movement of the 1950s and 1960s. Perhaps most important, the story of "Strange Fruit" demonstrates what can be accomplished when like-minded people focus their talents and energies on a common goal, and harness the power of art to create something far greater than themselves.

BILLIE HOLIDAY

BILLIE HOLIDAY lived a rich and remarkable life, darkened by difficulties but also made bright by her many great successes as a musical artist. As a black woman, her accomplishments were all the more extraordinary given the times in which she lived.

Billie was born Eleanora Fagan in 1915. Her father, a jazz guitarist, was not a part of her early life (she met him many years later), and her mother left her in the care of different relatives as she traveled to find work. As a girl, Billie was often in trouble with the law and was even sent to prison for several months at the age of 14. Fortunately, by then she had already heard the music of Louis Armstrong (jazz) and Bessie Smith (blues), experiences that changed her life and inspired her to sing.

By 1929, Billie was living with her mother in New York City, a vibrant world of music and the newest jazz. In small clubs and cafes, she began to work the floor, singing at customers' tables for tips and playing with her voice to make each song sound slightly different time after time. This was what made jazz unique and exciting—the spirit of *improvisation* that Billie learned from listening to trumpet and saxophone players change their solos to keep a song interesting and alive. When Billie was 17, respected music producer John Hammond heard her sing in Harlem and recognized her talents. He called her a "jazz genius" and helped her begin a recording career.

Even in her early records ("I Cried for You," for example), Billie used her voice to connect the melody of a song with the feeling behind the words. The quality of her sound—and the emotions she conveyed—soon led to hit songs and work with bandleaders like Count Basie and Teddy Wilson. She also became friends with jazz greats Lester Young (saxophone) and Ella Fitzgerald (vocals), and in 1938—at only 22—Billie was hired by Artie Shaw as one of the first black women to sing with an all-white band. There, her exposure to segregation and prejudice, particularly in the southern United States, made her keenly aware of racial injustice. When she came to Cafe Society and sang "Strange Fruit" in early 1939, Billie began to understand the power of song to provoke outrage, encourage change, and inspire healing.

In the 1940s, Billie achieved great popular success and came to be regarded as a *supreme vocalist*, someone whose musical style was imitated and admired by other, younger singers. She won many top jazz polls, acted in movies, and wrote some of her own songs. Sadly, as Billie's fame increased, so did her use of alcohol and drugs. After a short period of time in prison, she returned to great popular and critical acclaim, but her health had already begun to suffer.

By the time Billie died—in 1959, at the age of 44—she was considered one of the greatest female vocalists and jazz singers of all time. While the difficulties of her life played a part in her death, those painful experiences also made it possible for Billie to perform with a depth of feeling that makes her work unforgettable. Many people have tried to sing "Strange Fruit" with as much power and tenderness, but few have come close.

"She gave a startling, most dramatic and effective interpretation, which could jolt an audience out of its complacency anywhere. . . . This was exactly what I wanted the song to do and why I wrote it."

Abel Meeropol,
songwriter and activist

SOURCE NOTES

"Somebody once said . . ."
Billie Holiday with William Dufty, *Lady Sings the Blues*, 50th anniversary ed. (New York: Harlem Moon, 2006), 180.

"There was nothing like it . . ."
Barney Josephson wrote: "I wanted a club where blacks and whites worked together behind the footlights and sat together out front, a club whose stated advertised policy would be just that. There wasn't, so far as I know, a place like that in New York, or in the whole country for that matter."

Barney Josephson with Terry Trilling-Josephson, *Cafe Society: The Wrong Place for the Right People* (Urbana: University of Illinois Press, 2009), 9.

Both Barney and Abel were believers in what was called Negro liberation, a movement supported by groups like the National Association for the Advancement of Colored People (NAACP), to address racism and to promote greater legal and social equality for black people.

"The son of Jewish immigrants, Abel was outraged . . ."
Some researchers have noted that Abel Meeropol set the words of "Strange Fruit" to music only four days after Kristallnacht, the Night of Broken Glass, a planned series of attacks on Jewish people in Germany and Austria carried out by Nazi troops on November 9 to 10, 1938.

"Haunted for days by a photo . . ."
Abel Meerpol said: "Way back in the early Thirties, I saw a photograph of a lynching published in a magazine devoted to the exposure and elimination of racial injustice. It was a shocking photograph and haunted me for days. As a result, I wrote 'Strange Fruit' . . . [and later] set it to music."

Nancy Kovaleff Baker, "Abel Meeropol (a.k.a. Lewis Allan): Political Commentator and Social Conscience," *American Music* 20, no. 1 (Spring 2002): 45.

There is a widespread—but unproven—belief that the photograph Abel Meeropol saw was Lawrence Beitler's photo of a lynching in Marion, Indiana, on August 7, 1930. The victims of that event were Thomas Shipp (age 18) and Abram Smith (age 19). To view the photograph and read more about this lynching, see "Strange Fruit: Anniversary of a Lynching," *Radio Diaries*, NPR, August 6, 2010, http://www.npr.org/templates/story/story.php?storyId=129025516.

"For a few moments . . ."
"The first time Billie sang, part of it was this staging in a nightclub, it was like a bomb is dropped from some height. Before it can burst there's a slight split second. That's what happened the first time. Silence. Absolute silence. And then—boom! This big explosion. The audience really exploded, to the point where they rose to applaud. It was a terrific thing."

Josephson, *Cafe Society*, 48.

"But you'll be dead . . ."
David Margolick, *Strange Fruit: Billie Holiday, Café Society, and an Early Cry for Civil Rights* (Philadelphia: Running Press, 2000), 47.

"Billie referred to, Strange Fruit, as her personal protest . . ."
Holiday with Dufty, *Lady Sings the Blues*, 94.

"Nearly five thousand lynchings . . ."
"Lynchings: By Year and Race," University of Missouri-Kansas City, accessed June 27, 2015, http://law2.umkc.edu/faculty/projects/ftrials/shipp/lynchingyear.html.

"She gave a startling . . ."
Abel Meeropol quoted in Margolick, *Strange Fruit*, 46.

"People had to remember 'Strange Fruit' . . ."
Barney Josephson quoted in Dorian Lynskey, "Strange Fruit: The First Great Protest Song," *Guardian* (US edition), February 16, 2011, https://www.theguardian.com/music/2011/feb/16/protest-songs-billie-holiday-strange-fruit.

SELECTED BIBLIOGRAPHY

Greene, Meg. *Billie Holiday: A Biography*. Westport, CT: Greenwood Press, 2007.

Holiday, Billie. *Billie Holiday*. New York: Verve, 2011. compact disc.

———. *Billie Holiday: The Commodore Master Takes*. New York: GRP Records, 2000. compact disc.

Holiday, Billie, with William Dufty. *Lady Sings the Blues*. 50th anniversary ed. New York: Harlem Moon, 2006.

Josephson, Barney, with Terry Trilling-Josephson. *Cafe Society: The Wrong Place for the Right People*. Urbana: University of Illinois Press, 2009.

Margolick, David. *Strange Fruit: Billie Holiday, Café Society, and an Early Cry for Civil Rights*. Philadelphia: Running Press, 2000.

Strange Fruit. DVD. Directed and produced by Joel Katz. San Francisco: California Newsreel, 2002.

Weatherford, Carole Boston. *Becoming Billie Holiday*. Honesdale, PA: Wordsong, 2008.

Search online to find a video of Billie Holiday singing "Strange Fruit," live in London, England, in 1959.